Lots of Ladybugs!

Counting by Fives

Special thanks to our advisers for their expertise:

Stuart Farm, M.Ed., Mathematics Lecturer
University of North Dakota, Grand Forks

Susan Kesselring, M.A., Literacy Educator
Rosemount-Apple Valley-Eagan (Minnesota) School District

by Michael Dahl   illustrated by Todd Ouren

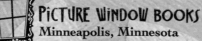

PICTURE WINDOW BOOKS
Minneapolis, Minnesota

Managing Editor: Catherine Neitge
Creative Director: Terri Foley
Art Director: Keith Griffin
Editor: Christianne Jones
Designer: Todd Ouren
Page production: Picture Window Books
The illustrations in this book were prepared digitally.

Picture Window Books
1710 Roe Crest Drive
North Mankato, MN 56003
www.capstonepub.com

Library of Congress Cataloging-in-Publication Data
Dahl, Michael.
Lots of ladybugs! : counting by fives / written by Michael
Dahl ; illustrated by Todd Ouren.
p. cm. — (Know your numbers)
ISBN-13: 978-1-4048-0944-4 (hardcover)
ISBN-13: 978-1-4048-1118-8 (paperback)
1. Counting—Juvenile literature. 2. Multiplication—Juvenile
literature. 3. Ladybugs—Juvenile literature. I. Ouren, Todd,
ill. II. Title.

QA113.D337 2005
513.2'11—dc22   2004019003

Printed in the United States   5188